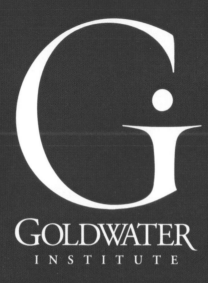

GOLDWATER
INSTITUTE

A Project of the Van Sittert Center for Constitutional
Advocacy at the Goldwater Institute

Printed by BookBaby.com

A Is for the American Dream

Written by Amelia Hamilton
with Matt Beienburg
Illustrated by Anthony Resto

A

is for the American Dream.

America is a land of opportunity, where anyone can succeed, no matter their beginnings. In America, we all have the freedom to pursue our own dream.
What is your American Dream?

B is for Bravery.

Bravery means being strong even when we are afraid or face challenges. Americans have bravely explored, founded, and defended the United States so that we can be free. It takes bravery to achieve your American Dream.

C is for Constitution.

America's founders wrote down important rules in the Constitution. The Constitution protects us from tyrants and other bullies, and it keeps us free to follow our dreams.

July 4, 1776.

ATION

A

D is for Declaration of Independence.

In 1776, America's founders dreamed of a new nation where we all have the right to life, liberty, and the pursuit of happiness. They wrote the Declaration of Independence to tell the world about it.

E is for Education.

Education teaches us about our country's history and heroes. We learn at school, at home, in books, and in the world around us. Education gives us the skills we need to achieve our dreams.

F is for Freedom.

Freedom means having the power to make decisions without being told what to do. The Constitution safeguards our freedom to speak, worship, protect our families, and pursue our American Dream.

G is for Gratitude.

When we have gratitude, we are thankful for the good things we have. We should be grateful to live in a free country and grateful for the people who have fought to protect it.

H is for Hard Work.

It's not easy to achieve the American Dream. It takes a lot of hard work to build your dreams from the ground up. But with time, you can reach the sky.

I is for Inventor.

Inventors dream about new things no one else ever imagined. In America, kids like you have grown up to invent cars, airplanes, computers, and so much more. What is something you would like to invent?

J is for Justice.

In America, justice means that laws and rules are the same for everyone. It doesn't matter whether you are rich or poor or what the color of your skin is.

Every adult was once a kid like you, with a dream about what they would be when they grew up. Someday, you will have a chance to live and protect the American Dream, just like the grown-ups in your life have done for you!

L is for Liberty.

Throughout history, people have not been free. Millions have come to America and helped make it a land where there is freedom and liberty for all.

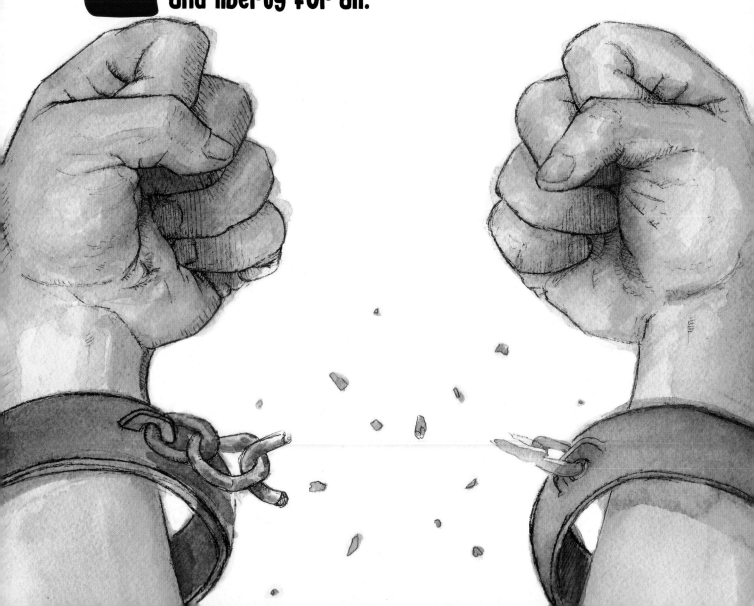

M is for Merit.

Merit means practicing, studying, and working hard to be good at what we do. In America, we celebrate each other's merits, and you can earn applause, a gold medal, or a prize for what you achieve.

N is for Nation.

A nation is a large group of people who share something in common. America is a nation of 50 states and millions of people who share a love of freedom and who all have dreams of their own.

O is for Opportunity.

In America, we all have equal opportunity – the power to pursue our American Dream. Where we end up depends not on where we start, but on where we decide to go.

P is for Prosperity.

Prosperity means that we can live a good life and earn money for the things we need – and want – if we work hard. Thanks to our freedoms, every American can prosper and thrive.

Q is for Quest.

From exploring the rivers and mountains of the west, to going on a mission to the moon, Americans have always dreamed of new quests to push themselves farther than before. What is your quest?

R is for Republic.

Thanks to the founders who wrote the Constitution, America is a republic. Each of us holds the power to help decide how our country works. We get to choose people to make our laws.

S is for Statue of Liberty.

The Statue of Liberty stands in New York Harbor. It is a symbol of the American Dream all across the country and all around the world. It has welcomed new people to follow their dreams for more than 100 years.

 **is for Talent.**

Talent, education, and hard work are the secret combination that will help you succeed in making your American Dream come true. Your talent makes you stand out and opens the doors to new opportunities. What is your special talent?

U is for United States.

The United States is more than just a name – it's exactly what we are: 50 states united together. Each state is a unique place where every person can achieve their dreams, and no state gets bossed around.

V is for Vote.

Voting gives us a say in how our country works. In many places around the world, people dream of being able to vote. Voting protects our ability to achieve our dreams. What would you vote to protect or make better?

W is for Washington, D.C.

Congress and the President are in Washington, D.C. But it's important to remember that they are only in charge of a few things. This country is so big and has so many different people that letting each state be different is the best way for everyone to achieve their dream.

When you do your best and shine, you can be rewarded for excellence. America celebrates people who excel. Our country's national anthem, "The Star-Spangled Banner," sings proudly of America's excellence.

ON THIS DAY WE PROUDLY RECOGNIZE THE NEW OWNER
OF THE AMERICAN DREAM

Thank you for choosing America

Signature _____

Y is for YOU.

The American Dream is for you, whether you're rich and famous or come from the most humble beginnings. In America, every single person can achieve a dream of their own.

Z is for Zeal.

Are you excited about your dreams? It may take a lot of hard work to make your dreams come true, but follow those dreams with zeal and passion – and don't give up! That can take you all the way to success.

Author
Amelia Hamilton

Amelia Hamilton is a writer and historian who is passionate about advancing liberty. She has a master's degree in both English and 18th-century history from the University of St Andrews in Scotland and a postgraduate diploma in fine and decorative arts from Christie's, London.

Amelia loves hockey, old movies, apple juice, and her labrador Myrtle.

Author
Matt Beienburg

Matt Beienburg is the Director of Education Policy at the Goldwater Institute. He also serves as director of the Institute's Van Sittert Center for Constitutional Advocacy.

A native of Arizona, Matt earned a bachelor's in economics from Claremont McKenna College and a master's in public affairs from Princeton.

Artist
Anthony Resto

After completing his bachelor's degree at the American Academy of Art, Anthony has worked with various publishing companies and independent authors to create books, logo designs, and storyboards. He now teaches art full time as well as illustrating.

The Goldwater Institute

The Goldwater Institute is the nation's preeminent liberty organization and is committed to empowering all Americans to live freer, happier lives. Learn more at GoldwaterInstitute.org.

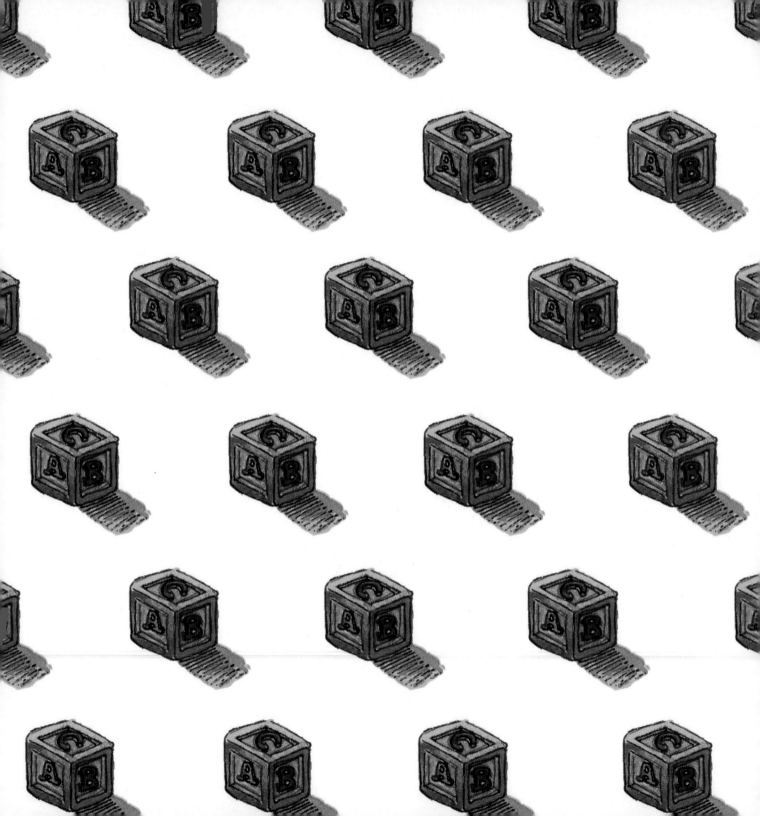